SOUTH CENTRAL STORIES.

DOUBLE OR NOTHIN'
THE RIDE
HAPPY ANNIVERSARY, PUNK!

MICHAEL AJAKWE, JR.

SOUTH CENTRAL STORIES:

DOUBLE OR NOTHIN'
THE RIDE
HAPPY ANNIVERSARY, PUNK!

Excerpts from Michael Ajakwe, Jr.'s *Double or Nothin'*
appear in *Best Men's Stage Monologues* 1996 (Smith &
Krause*)*, *Best Stage Scenes 1996*, and *Outstanding Stage
Monologs & Scenes of the 90s* (Merriweather). Excerpts
from *Happy Anniversary, Punk!* appear in *Best Men's Stage
Monologues 1996* and *Outstanding Stage Monologs &
Scenes of the '90's*. Excerpts from *The Ride* appear in the
A&E documentary series *Minute by Minute: The O.J.
Simpson/Al Cowlings Bronco Chase* (June 2001). His cor-
porate novel *Company Policy* (Pipedream Press) was nom-
inated for three NAACP Theater Awards in 1994—Best
Actor, Best Actress and Best Playwright (Ajakwe won the
latter). Excerpts have appeared in *Best Men's Stage
Monologues 1995* and *Best Women's Stage Monologues
1995*. In 1997, Ajakwe won a second NAACP Theater
Award, this time as Best Producer for *Love Boat* star-
turned-playwright Ted Lange's *Four Queens, No Trump!* A
former segment producer for *Entertainment Tonight*, he
won an Emmy in 1995 as a producer for E! Network's *Talk
Soup* and has written for hit shows like *Martin, Between
Brothers, Sister Sister, The Brothers Garcia, Moesha, The
Parkers* and *Soul Food*. Ajakwe also teaches television
writing at the University of Southern California in the Bill
Cosby-sponsored Guy Hanks/Marvin Miller TV &
Screenwriting Program. He lives in View Park, California.

Other published plays by MICHAEL AJAKWE, JR.

Company Policy
(Pipedream Press, February 2000/
Millennium Collector's Edition, March 2001)

SOUTH CENTRAL STORIES:

DOUBLE OR NOTHIN'
THE RIDE
HAPPY ANNIVERSARY, PUNK!

Acknowledgements

I'd like to send a shout out to Tony Bracy, who I first heard use the term "south central stories" on a tennis court ten years ago, for "allowing me" to use his title. I also want to recognize Regina Davis Evans, Al Schaben and Maurice Oldham whose photographs appear on the cover. Big ups to Stan Peters at Pipedream Press for believing in my work, and Big Jae Prosser at Omega Graphics for his expertise, patience and creativity. Lastly, I want to thank my ace boon Howard Love, and his son Chance. I would've never gotten through the original run without you two.

Michael Ajakwe, Jr.

SOUTH CENTRAL STORIES:

DOUBLE OR NOTHIN'
THE RIDE
HAPPY ANNIVERSARY, PUNK!

―――――――――――

THREE PLAYS BY

MICHAEL AJAKWE, JR.

PIPEDREAM PRESS
A DIVISION OF PIPEDREAM PRODUCTIONS, INC.   LOS ANGELES

PIPEDREAM ORIGINAL
FIRST EDITION, MARCH 2001

All inquiries concerning performance rights for *South Central
Stories* should be addressed to Pipedream Press, 3717 S. LaBrea
Avenue, Suite 530, Los Angeles, California 90016 800-550-4191.
Website: *Pipedreampress.com* E-mail: Pipedreampress@aol.com

ISBN 0-9678579-2-9
Library of Congress Catalog Card Number: 2001116949

DOUBLE OR NOTHIN'

Double or Nothin' began performances August 5, 1994 at the Masquers Café Theater, West Los Angeles. Harris Smith, Artistic Director. Michael Ajakwe, Jr., Howard Love, Executive Producers.

The play was cast as follows:

	First Cast	Second Cast
FRANK	Howard Love	NONE
CHANCE	Chance Love	NONE
SHERRY	Fawn Reed	Tyna Andrews

Anthony Bracy, the associate producer, designed the set and lights; Mark Laurent designed the sound; Tyna Andrews provided the choreography. The director was Michael Ajakwe, Jr.

On April 12, 1996, *Double or Nothin'* was revived at the Hudson Theater in Hollywood, California, as a part of *Three African-American One-Acts*. Spencer Scott and Darron Johnson played Frank, while Robert Ri'chard and Richard Atkins shared the Chance role. Kimberlee Furgess and Taffye Wallace were each played Sherry. Rochelle Cunningham, Marc Lewis, Christopher Williams and Devika Parikh performed in the opening dance sequence. The director was Michael Edwards.

THE RIDE

On April 12, 1996, *The Ride* began performances at the Hudson Mainstage Theater as a part of *Three African-American One-Acts*. Elizabeth Reilly, Gary Blumsack, Jack Stehlin, Artistic Directors. Michael Ajakwe, Jr., Executive Producer.

The play was cast as follows:

	<u>First Cast</u>	<u>Second Cast</u>
O.J. SIMPSON	Phil Morris	Gary Simpson
AL COWLINGS	Bill Overton	Gary Simpson
VOICE OVER	Carl Gilliard	NONE

Mark Laurent designed the sound; Kathie O'Donohue designed the lights; Marco De Leon designed the set; Robert Taylor designed and built the white Bronco; Helena Jackson stage managed with assistance from Kristen Payne; Andre Grayson back-stage managed with assistance from Howard and Chance Love. Michael Ajakwe, Jr. was the director.

HAPPY ANNIVERSARY, PUNK!

On April 12, 1996, *Happy Anniversary, Punk!* began performances at the Hudson Theater as a part of *Three African-American One-Acts*.   Elizabeth Reilly, Gary Blumsack, Jack Stehlin, Artistic Directors.   Michael Ajakwe, Jr., Executive Producer.

The cast was as follows:

	First Cast	Second Cast	Third Cast
AL	Tommy Hicks	Lou Beatty, Jr.	Ted Lange
BIG MAC	Al Garrett	Desean Terry	NONE

Mark Laurent designed the sound; Kathie O'Donohue designed the lights; Marco De Leon designed the set; Helena Jackson stage managed wih assistance from Kristen Payne; Andre Grayson back-stage managed with assistance from Howard and Chance Love. The director was Ted Lange.

PRODUCTION NOTES

South Central Stories

In Los Angeles, anything that takes place south of Wilshire Boulevard, whether it occurs in Inglewood or Gardena or Compton, Hawthorne, LaDera Heights or Baldwin Hills— if it happens where Black folk live, it's "south central." Well, this book celebrates stuff that goes down on the Black side of LA's Mason/Dixon Line; my personal tribute to that faceless part of town the media loves to call "south central LA."

Double or Nothin'

I wrote this play during a time in my life when it seemed every other woman I went out with had a child or two... or three. I wrote it for fun, with no real intent of having it produced. In fact, each time the play was staged, it was at the urging of others.

The first was Harris Smith, who ran Masquers Theater in West LA. Harris had learned that *Company Policy* was enjoying a successful run at the Hudson and contacted me. He was willing to forgo charging a rental fee if I staged a play at Masquers. Since the theater rental is often a producer's biggest expense, Harris' offer was one I couldn't refuse.

The pre-production window was short—just three weeks. Rather than endure an exhaustive casting call, I chose to rely on actors I already knew. The child in the play, Chance, was named after my producing partner's eight year old son. Although we were partners, Howard Love was also the lead in many of my productions and my first choice to originate the role of Frank in *Double or Nothin'*. Howard always wanted to work with his son

Chance on stage, so when the Masquers opportunity presented itself, I cast Chance in his namesake role. Fawn Reed was the wife of a high school classmate. She was a print model, statuesque and stunning, who was trying to make the transition to acting. After she read with Howard and Chance, I cast her as the object of Frank's desire, Sherry. Tyna Andrews, an amazing dancer and the niece of a friend, was brought in to choreograph the opening dance sequence. Like Fawn, Tyna was also transitioning to acting. So, in exchange for her choreography, she understudied Fawn.

Double or Nothin' opened at Masquers on August 4, 1994 and had a six-week run.

Double or Nothin' was staged the second time at the urging of a close friend. Arthur Anderson and I have known each other since high school. I went off to college and Art started a carpet cleaning business. He has since turned in his steam vac for a real estate license and is somewhat of a mini-mogul in south central. Early in my career, Art would read a lot of my work and offer feedback. When I was ready to stage two of my one-acts in 1996 and Art learned that *Double or Nothin'* was not among them, he went to bat for it. My reservation was simple. Unlike *Double or Nothin'*, the other plays were dramas. At Art's prodding, I included *Double or Nothin'* and *A Tale of Two One-Acts* became *3 African-American One-Acts*. Art's suggestion turned out to be one of the best career moves I've ever made. Besides being a crowd pleaser, *Double or Nothin'* is arguably my most celebrated play to date, having appeared in *Best Men's Monologues 1996, Best Stage Scenes 1996* and *Outstanding Stage Monologs & Scenes of the 90's*. Who knew? I didn't. Thanks Art!

When I decided to include *Double or Nothin'* in the Hudson production, the first person I called was Wendy Raquel Robinson. I had met Wendy, coincidentally, through Art. She and I have known each other since 1989, when she was a promising Howard University senior with dreams of graduating and becoming a star. Years later, she would become one of the stars of *The Steve Harvey Show*. I wanted Wendy to both direct and star in *Double or Nothin'*, but she was doing a play of her own at her theater company, Amazing Grace Conservatory, and had to decline. I also approached Renee Tenison about playing Sherry. I worked with Renee, 1990 *Playboy* Playmate of The Year, on *Martin*. She expressed an interest in doing theater so I sent her the play. I never heard back from Renee.

Except for Darron Johnson, who I already had in mind to play Frank, the other actors were pulled from casting calls. I found my two Sherrys, the alluring Taffye Wallace and loveable Kimberlee Furgess, at auditions held at the Hudson, as well as my second Frank, Spencer Scott. Richard Atkins, an adorable pint-sized nine-year old, was picked to play Chance from a group of kids I auditioned at Wendy's theater company, AGC. But my biggest catch came when I visited Faith Acting Studios, a wonderful acting school for inner-city kids. That's where I first saw Robert Ri'chard. Though too old for the role, this 12-year old so blew me away with his charm and ability I cast him as Chance anyway, making the character 10 instead of eight during his performances. Young Robert went on to win an Emmy the next year opposite Louis Gossett, Jr. in the Showtime movie *In My Father's Name*, has starred in the film *Light It Up* with Forrest Whitaker, and had his own series, *Cousin Skeeter*, on Nickelodeon. I also managed to recruit Robert's talented acting coach, Michael Edwards, to direct the production.

Double or Nothin' opened at the Hudson Mainstage on April 12, 1996 and ran for six-weeks.

On the surface, *Double or Nothin'* is about dating, but its subtext is family. Chance is a terror, not because he's spoiled but because he's angry due to the absence of his dad in his life. Like so many other Black boys, underneath all that attitude is pain.

Frank, who is probably a struggling singer, is initially interested in just dating Sherry. But after encountering her "baggage," he has a decision to make—stay or run. The choice he makes indicates that his intentions transcend the casual. But Chance makes him pay dearly for it. Frank's challenge is patience and wisdom.

Sherry is a hard-working single mom looking for a good man with a job who likes kids. But her top priority is her son. She knows he's a piece of work but believes her soul mate will figure out a way to love them both.

Double or Nothin' runs 30 minutes with no intermission.

The Ride

I don't care what anybody says, nothing on television in my 35 years on this earth compares to that Bronco chase involving O.J. Simpson and the Santa Ana and Orange County police departments. Minute for minute, I challenge ANYONE to find a more compelling piece of TV. After the slow-speed chase, everything else that followed that media circus felt almost anti-climactic.

The idea for this play sprang from a question. What is the biggest mystery of the Nicole Brown/Ron Goldman tragedy? Answer: Did O.J. Simpson commit these terrible murders? (Though acquitted of the crime, polls show that most Americans believe O.J. did kill his ex-wife.) The second biggest mystery of the case? Answer: What did O.J. and A.C. talk about in that Bronco? Since I didn't feel comfortable revisiting the grizzly crime scene, I chose to focus on that infamous pursuit. I felt, and still feel, historians will debate it for years.

When I got the idea for *The Ride*, I didn't have time to write it because I had just been hired on *Martin*. So I did something I'd never done before. I invested in a tape recorder and began dictating the piece on my way to and from work at stoplights. Thus, *The Ride* was actually written while I was, well, riding. (I still have the micro-cassette to prove it.)

After I wrote *The Ride*, I did a reading at my house with Howard Love and Darron Johnson that convinced me it was worth staging. Though two of my favorite actors, Howard and Darron were both too young for the roles. Since the events were so recent, I felt the actors should resemble the real life characters. To not do so, in my opinion, would be a distraction for the audience.

From the beginning, there was only one actor I thought of to play O.J.—Phil Morris. Most of America knows Phil as Kramer's fast-talking attorney Jackie Chiles on *Seinfeld*. (Ironically, the character is a satire of O.J.'s lead attorney Johnny Cochran). Not only does Phil look like a young O.J., he's a much better actor. I didn't know Phil, but I did know his sister Iona, who put me in touch with him. He read *The Ride* and was on board.

I saw veteran actor Richard Lawson in the A.C. role. I didn't know Richard, but my then-girlfriend playwright/entrepreneur Angela de Joseph, had a good friend who did. Richard, who just so happens to be a pal of O.J. and A.C.'s, read the piece and passed.

I thought of Laurence Hilton-Jacobs, Freddie "Boom Boom" Washington from the *Welcome Back Kotter* TV series. I'd admired his work since he played Cochese in *Cooley High* and feel he's one of the most underrated actors in the business. Angela got his number from a friend and I called him. Larry couldn't do *The Ride* because he was already committed to another project.

I needed an A.C. more than O.J. ever did, but I couldn't just cast anyone. In some ways, the role is more critical than the O.J. role since A.C. was, in essence, the hostage negotiator. I also needed someone who could hold his own with a real pro like Phil Morris.

As I was trying to figure out what to do, Phil phoned me wondering if I'd found an A.C. I said I was working on it. That's when he suggested Cylk Cozart. Cylk, who'd co-starred in *White Men Can't Jump!*, would be an ideal A.C., first of all, because he looked a lot like him. He was also a solid performer. Phil gave me Cylk's number, we talked, I sent him the piece, he read it and was down.

Mission accomplished, right? Wrong. Cylk got work on an Arnold Schwarzeneggar film called *Erasure* and had to regretfully bow out the week before rehearsals were to begin. Now, I was really in a pinch. That's when I remembered Bill Overton.

Bill was an old friend who, along with his celebrity actress/wife Jayne Kennedy, had optioned a screenplay of mine six years prior. The movie never got made but Bill and I and Jayne became friends. I never considered him initially because, although Bill began in this business as a model/actor, he had long ago traded in his SAG card to become a producer. But when I thought about it, he would be even better for the A.C. role than Cylk because he not only resembled the real-life A.C., they were the same age. My problem now was coaxing Bill out of retirement. Fortunately, after he read *The Ride*, he obliged me. Finally, I had my leads. Whew!

Since I'm a firm believer in double casting, I held auditions prior to rehearsals to find someone to understudy Bill and Phil. Since O.J. and A.C. slightly resemble each other, I was hoping to find one guy who looked enough like O.J., but then again could be mistaken for A.C. too. I honestly didn't think I would find that guy, but I did. His name was Gary Simpson. Not only was Gary the perfect back up, he was also a perfect gentleman, just a pleasure to work with.

In fact, working with this cast of actors has been my most satisfying experience as a director. Everyone was so giving, not just to me but to each other. They really dug deep, searched their souls to make their performances ring true, and made me very proud. They were consummate professionals and served as role models to the actors in the other two plays.

The Ride opened at the Hudson Mainstage on April 12, 1996 and ran for six-weeks.

I must commend Robert Taylor for the amazing Bronco he built. The choice to actually recreate the vehicle on stage rather than just have the actors in bucket seats or chairs really captured the immediacy of the event, giving the play a real life feel. Thank you, Robert.

I purposely chose not to distort the fact that O.J. views himself as a victim. A.C., on the other hand, serves as a mouthpiece for us, the public. He gets to ask O.J. many of the questions he never answered during the trial since he didn't take the stand. I feel whoever performs *The Ride* should not use it to promote an agenda. Judgment should be left to the audience. That's what makes it a play and not propaganda.

The Ride runs 40-45 minutes without an intermission.

Happy Anniversary Punk!

I wrote this play for Charles Dutton. It was inspired by a real-life tragedy that I had read about in "the Black bible," *Jet*. It was about a 22-year old professional football player who had been gunned down by a teenager at a Cincinnati club over a parking space. It immediately reminded me of all the times I'd heard or read about Black people killing each other over stupid shit. Stuff that didn't mean anything. It made me so damn mad. Shane Curry had his whole future in front of him. Just the year prior, the former University of Miami defensive end was the Indianapolis Colt's top draft pick. Shane was engaged and a soon-to-be father. But on May 3, 1992, he officially became a statistic—another casualty of Black-on-Black crime.

Whenever a minor commits a violent crime in this country, public sentiment tends to fall on the perpetrator rather than the victim. Being a minor seems to automatically dismiss the act as mindless instead of malicious. Everybody wants to rehabilitate the child, forgetting that a life has been lost. I wanted to tell the story of teen violence from the point of view of the bereaved. I initially wanted to call the piece *The Parent Strikes Back* but soon settled on *Happy Anniversary, Punk!* I felt the only actor who could truly do the play justice was Charles "Roc" Dutton. Unfortunately, I didn't know him. No one I knew knew him either. So I went the conventional route by contacting his manager. I wrote several letters, phoned repeatedly for nearly a year but never got a response. Though disappointed, I had no choice but to move on.

I'd gone to see Laurence Fishburne in a play he wrote and directed called *Riff Raff*. After the play, I congratulated Laurence and told him I had a piece I was planning to mount that I felt he could really sink his teeth into. He told me to contact his manager and gave me her card. I called and wrote his manager for six months but never got a response. Again, I moved on.

I thought Art Evans could play Al Fletcher. Art is one of the best character actors in town. He's also funny and the role needed an actor adept at both comedy and drama. I also felt the role would be more interesting with an actor who didn't look necessarily menacing. Sometimes, the scariest people are those who appear the least threatening, like Alan Bates in *Psycho*. My then-girlfriend Angela was doing a staged reading at the Richard Pryor Theater (now The Hollywood Playhouse) on Las Palmas and Art was in it. After a rehearsal, I approached him. He dug the premise and asked to read the play. A few days later, we talked. Art loved it. Wanted to do it. There was only one problem. During the run, he would be out of town shooting *Metro* with Eddie Murphy. Let's see... Eddie Murphy, me. Eddie Murphy, me. Hmm...that's a tough one. (Art and I would work at the Zephyr in 1999 when I produced my then-girlfriend Christina Harley's play *The Dreamers*.)

After Art chose Eddie, I went to see a play at a theater in Liemert Park that was owned by Marla Gibbs of the old *Jeffersons* series. *Dink's Blues* starred Dick Anthony Williams. I've been a fan of Dick's since his show-stopping performance as Pretty Tony in the pimp classic *The Mack*. That old saying, 'there are no small roles, just small actors,' certainly applies to him. Dick's one of those actors who's good in everything he does. After I saw him tear up *Dink's Blues*, I thought he'd make a great Al. Dick read the piece and was interested but didn't feel comfortable juggling two shows, since *Dink's Blues* would still be running during my run. I respected his decision and, once again, moved on.

I decided to switch gears and look for a director. First person I thought of was Denise Dowse. Denise is one of the best theater directors in town and a nice person. Landing her would've been be a major coup. Unfortunately for me, Denise had already committed to direct Angela's play, *The Chest*.

My next choice was Justin Lord. A year earlier, I'd seen Justin direct a staged reading of the play *Rapture* by Jocelyn Luckett at the Stella Adler Theater in Hollywood. I was impressed with his technique and felt a director with his gifts could only enhance the piece. Justin read *Happy Anniversary, Punk!* and was in.

Justin suggested we hold an open call to find our Al. We saw a number of fine actors but the three who stood out were Tommy Hicks, Bill Brown and Lou Beatty, Jr. I'd wanted to work with Tommy for ten years, ever since I saw him in Spike Lee's debut film *She's Gotta Have It!* His audition was a formality, as far as I was concerned, and an honor. Choosing the second Al was much tougher. Bill was moving. I knew he could make the audience feel his pain, which was very important. But Justin wanted Lou and I couldn't blame him. If you've never met Lou, you're missing something. This guy not only has chops, he's got a James Earl Jones voice to match. My only reservation was the very thing that makes Lou special—his power. I wondered if the audience would sympathize with him. Justin felt he could alleviate my concern and Lou got the part. (I would work with Bill years later in *The Dreamers*).

We found one of our Big Macs at Faith Acting Studio. Desean Terry was very green. But what he lacked in experience he made up for in raw talent. There was something about Desean that rung true. It also helped that, like the character in the play, he really was 15. We found our other Big Mac at AGC. Al Garrett looked 16 but I heard a rumor he was 21. Didn't matter. Al had so much ability it was scary. He blew away all the other kids we auditioned. This was one choice Justin and I were in complete agreement on.

Just when it seemed the worst was behind me, more trouble. Mid-way through rehearsals, Justin and I had creative differences over an element he wanted to add to the play. Though I had the utmost respect for his vision, I disagreed with this particular suggestion. Now, Justin's a Libra. So am I. Libras can be some stubborn folks sometimes. Justin stood his ground, I stood mine and we parted ways. Because we're both professionals, however, we remained civil and, to this day, are friends.

Even though I was directing *The Ride*, I decided to step in and finish what Justin had started. First person I called was Tommy Hicks. Tommy really wanted to work with Justin. I thought he might quit when he found out Justin was out. To my surprise (and blessing), he didn't. He did feel it was a bad idea for me to direct, considering all of my other responsibilities. And I knew he was right. He suggested Ted Lange, Isaac from the old *Love Boat* series. Tommy went over Ted's house that morning to loan him his copy of my play. Ted called me that night. He totally got my vision. But he had some ideas to strengthen Big Mac's character. It was basically the same thing Justin was saying only, instead of adding an action that would undermine the play's urgency, Ted's notes gave Big Mac dimension. So I took them. Ted stepped in and did an outstanding job. Tommy really saved my ass.

Happy Anniversary, Punk! opened at the Hudson Mainstage on April 12, 1996 and ran for six-weeks.

During the last week of the run, Tommy landed a paying gig and had to leave town. Lou, who had a pre-arranged engagement, was also out of town. So guess who had to play Al? Ted. And, man, did he work it. Ted and I became and remain good friends. The next year, we produced one of his plays, *Four Queens, No Trump!* Besides being a talented actor and director, Ted is one of the most prolific playwrights in America.

The key to this play is that the audience must believe Al can/will kill Big Mac. If you tip the ending too soon, you compromise the integrity of the story.

Happy Anniversary, Punk! runs 40-45 minutes with no intermission.

SOUTH CENTRAL STORIES:

DOUBLE OR NOTHIN'
THE RIDE
HAPPY ANNIVERSARY, PUNK!

To:

Michael Ajakwe, Sr. (July 26, 1934 – August 27, 2000)
If every child had a father like you, there'd be no
single moms, kid killers or fallen heroes.

&

Shane Clifton Curry (April 7, 1968 – May 3, 1992)
Your senseless murder was not in vain.

DOUBLE OR NOTHIN'

ACT I

Scene 1

SETTING: *A dance hall. Day.*

AT RISE: FRANK JOHNSON, *28, enters the room in a spotlight. The rest of the room is black.* FRANK *is singing (as best he can) the opening bar of the 1980 Rick James/Tina Marie classic "Fire and Desire".*

FRANK
(Singing)
"Love them and leave them... That's what I used to do... use and abuse them..."
(Beat; normal speak)
Until I met Sherry.
(Reminiscing)
I'll never forget it.

(Lights dim. Dance music fades up.

At the bar, on the other side of the room, a gorgeous woman, SHERRY, 29, is staring at what is now a packed dance floor, nursing a drink and watching the festivities.)

FRANK
She was just sitting there, all by her lonesome, having what looked like an M.C. Hammer but could've very well been a V-8. Now, normally, it ain't my style to ask a babe to dance,

specifically when she's thirty feet away, 'cause if I do and she says no <u>everybody</u> in the house is gonna know about it.

>*(A* GUY *moves across the room to ask* SHERRY *to dance. She stares him up and down like he's a Martian, shakes her head and looks away, leaving him high and dry. The* GUY *looks at the audience, embarrassed, and attempts to "casually" ease off stage.)*

FRANK

See. That could've been me — an accident waiting to happen.

>*(*SHERRY *makes eye contact with* FRANK. FRANK *looks around, unsure whether she's actually looking at him. He points to himself and she nods, then looks away.)*

FRANK

Yawl see that! Got her cold busted. And she didn't even try to hide it. Women... Yawl think yawl so slick. And you are. But one thing's for sure — when you wanna let a brother know what time it is, yawl don't waste no time.
>*(Beat)*
So what do yawl think? Should I "go for it"? Should I "make my move"? Or should I just straight up "bum-rush the show"?
>*(Off their looks)*
That means everything I just said.
>*(To a confused patron)*
What's the matter, ain't never lived in the ghetto before? I didn't think so.

(Setting his sights back on SHERRY*)*
I think I'm gonna go for it.
(Starts for the bar, then stops)
But if she turns me down, I'm kicking somebody's ass.

*(*SHERRY *looks at* FRANK *again. This time, he boldly, if not arrogantly, meets her stare. He slowly, coolly begins to approach. When he finally reaches her, he motions to the dance floor. She looks to the audience for her decision. On their approval, she puts her drink down and starts for the dance floor with an attitude thicker than molasses.* FRANK *follows her, throwing a "what'd I tell yawl" look at the audience. They meet on the dance floor in low gear, each trying to be oh so cool. Then* FRANK *busts a move and* SHERRY *busts back with a bigger move. This goes on and on — two magicians trying to outdo each other — until, in the end, they "chase" everyone off of the dance floor.* SHERRY *gets tired of competing with* FRANK *and storms off of the dance floor in a huff. Seeing this,* FRANK *begins jumping up and down like the heavyweight champion of the world. Then he realizes* SHERRY *has left and scrambles after her.)*

(Fade to black.)

(Fade music.)

FRANK
(Over black)
That's how I met the woman of my dreams.
(Beat)
After I turned her out on the dance floor, I caught up with her in the parking lot, got her number and told her I'd call her tomorrow. She said she'd be waiting.

<u>END OF SCENE 1</u>

ACT I

Scene 2

SETTING: SHERRY*'s living room. The next day.*

AT RISE: *SFX: Phone ringing. There is a sofa center stage, a coffee table, and a door stage left. SHERRY comes out, stage right, in her bathrobe and answers the phone.*

NOTE: FRANK *should be sitting in a chair with a cordless telephone, separate from the main set, front stage left.*

SHERRY

Hello?

FRANK

Sherry?

SHERRY

Speaking.

FRANK

This is Frank.

SHERRY

Who?

FRANK

Frank.

> SHERRY
>> *(Beat)*
>
> Frank who?

> FRANK
>
> Sinatra. I met you at the Funky Chicken last night.

> SHERRY
>
> I was there, but I don't remember meeting you, Mister Sinatra.

> FRANK
>
> Frank Johnson!
>> *(Beat)*
>
> I saw you at the bar... We <u>danced</u> together?

> SHERRY
>
> Oh, right, the brother who didn't know when to give in.

> FRANK
>
> You thought I was just gonna let you win? Uh-uh, baby, Frank Johnson will not be turned out by <u>anybody</u>. I'll take on Fred Astaire, Gene Kelly, the Nicholas Brothers. Bring 'em all on!

> SHERRY
>
> That is so stupid.

> FRANK
>> *(Ala Forrest Gump)*
>
> "Stupid is as stupid does."

> SHERRY
>
> All right "Forrest Gump".
>> *(Then)*
>
> How you doing?

> FRANK
>
> Fine now. I'll be even better when I see you again.

SHERRY

What are you doing tonight?

FRANK

Going over to your house.

SHERRY

Good. You can take me to dinner. I'll see you at seven sharp. Feel free to bring flowers. Or candy. Or money.

> *(SHERRY exits as we fade to black for FRANK's spotlight.)*

FRANK
> *(Beat, into phone)*

Hello...
> *(Beat)*

Hello?

> *(Kill spotlight.)*

END OF SCENE 2

ACT I

Scene 3

SETTING: SHERRY's living room.   That night.

AT RISE: CHANCE, 8, is sitting on the sofa playing a video game.

SFX: Knocking at the front door. CHANCE is too engrossed in his video game to care.

SFX: More knocking.

SHERRY (O.S.)
(Calling out)
Chance, would you get that for me?

CHANCE
(Calling back)
Who is it?

SHERRY (O.S.)
My date.

(CHANCE stops playing the game and looks up. A devilish grin soon covers his face.)

CHANCE
Don't worry, Mama, I'll take care of it.

(CHANCE puts down the video game and crosses to the door. He opens it, sees FRANK standing *there — flowers in one hand, a box of candy in the other, and a money clip in his mouth.   CHANCE reaches up, takes the money clip and slams the door in FRANK's face.   He starts back to the sofa, counting the money.)*

SFX: More knocking.)

SHERRY (O.S.)

Have you let that man in yet, Chance? Don't make me come out there and embarrass you.

(CHANCE reluctantly crosses back to the door again. FRANK is still standing there.   He looks pissed.)

CHANCE

Just playin', man.
(Giving him back the money)
Come on in.

(FRANK enters.)

FRANK

Who are you?

CHANCE

Who are you?

FRANK
(Taken aback)
Johnson. Mister Frank Johnson.

CHANCE

Have a seat... Frank.

(FRANK shoots him a look.
CHANCE starts back for the sofa.)

FRANK

Hang on. You didn't tell me your name.

CHANCE

Just call me The Man of the House.

(CHANCE sits down and resumes
playing his video game.)

SHERRY (O.S.)
(Calling out)

Hi, Frank!

FRANK
(Calling back)

How ya doin'?

SHERRY (O.S.)

Oh, fine. Did you meet Chance?

FRANK

No, I met "The Man".

SHERRY (O.S.)

Huh?

FRANK

I said, I like him. He's something else.

SHERRY (O.S.)

Isn't he? I'll be ready in a few minutes, okay?

FRANK

Take your time.

(FRANK sits next to CHANCE. He puts the box of candy on the living room table and leans back, holding the flowers. He takes in the place. CHANCE opens the box of candy and takes one. FRANK grabs his hand.)

FRANK

Those are for your mother.

CHANCE

My mother doesn't eat candy.

FRANK

But she said —

CHANCE

— "bring some candy." She always says that. And I always wind up eating it all 'cause she don't wanna get fat.

(FRANK looks at CHANCE for a long beat then releases his hand. CHANCE eats a piece of chocolate. He looks at FRANK and laughs.)

CHANCE

Sucker.

(FRANK grabs CHANCE by the collar.)

CHANCE

Touch me and I'll tell my mama.

(FRANK glares at CHANCE, eyes like hot coals, then releases him.)

                    FRANK

Little punk.

                    CHANCE
          (Cupping his ear)
Huh? I can't hear you. Speak up.

                         *(FRANK starts for him again,
                         ready to wring his neck.)*

                    CHANCE

Mama...!

                         *(FRANK covers his mouth, reduc-
                         ing CHANCE's pleas to mumbles.)*

                    FRANK
          (Whispering)
All right! All right! I'm... I'm sorry.

                         *(CHANCE finally calms down.
                         FRANK slowly removes his hand
                         from   CHANCE's   mouth.
                         CHANCE smiles, sardonically.)*

                    FRANK

You're a devil.

                    CHANCE

Don't you forget it.
          (Pointing)
Have my mama home by midnight or else.

                    FRANK

Or else, what? My car's gonna turn into a pumpkin?
          (Laughs at his own joke)

                    CHANCE

No, I'll call nine-one-one and say you kidnapped her.

FRANK

What?!

CHANCE

You heard me, sucker.

> (SHERRY *enters from her bed-room. She looks like a million bucks. She gives* FRANK *a big hug. As he spins her around,* FRANK *shoots* CHANCE *a sly victorious grin.* CHANCE *sits back on the sofa, arms folded, staring at* FRANK *the whole while. He's not a happy camper.* SHER-RY *looks at her watch and leads* FRANK *towards the door.)*

SHERRY

Let's go. I don't want to be late for the movie.

FRANK

What movie?

SHERRY

The movie you're taking me to <u>after</u> dinner.

> (SHERRY *exits.* FRANK *follows, turning back to* CHANCE *with a teasing tongue, before exiting.* CHANCE *stands, pointing.)*

CHANCE

Remember what I said, punk! Midnight or you're a fugitive!

> *(Black out.)*

<u>END OF SCENE 3</u>

<u>ACT I</u>

<u>Scene 4</u>

<u>SETTING</u>:   *SHERRY's living room.   Same night.*

<u>AT RISE</u>:   SHERRY *and* FRANK *enter.*

SHERRY
I can't believe we left before the end of the movie.

FRANK
Seen one flesh-eating monster, seen 'em all.
              (Aside, checking his watch)
Midnight.

SHERRY
You have someplace else to go?

FRANK
No, just checking.

SHERRY
Frank, we never found out who the killer was.

FRANK
What do you mean? It was the butler.

SHERRY
              (Unconvinced)
How do you know?

FRANK
Because, my dear Sherry, it's always the butler.
              (Breaking it down)

All these movies are the same, Sherry. The actors may be different, but those formula spots — those tired, Hollywood clichés — they never change.
> *(Off her look)*

Didn't I tell you that before the end of the movie the brother was gonna get killed?
> *(Off her nod)*

Stevie Wonder could've saw that coming.

> *(They cross to the sofa and sit.)*

SHERRY

I had a nice time.

FRANK

You did?

> *(SHERRY nods, moving closer.)*

FRANK

How nice?

SHERRY

Very nice.

FRANK

Nice as in "thanks for payin'" or nice as in "next time I'm treatin'"?

SHERRY
> *(Even closer)*

Nice as in "shut up and kiss me"!

FRANK

Yes, ma'am.

> *(They're about to kiss when they hear a loud yawn. FRANK looks around the room, confused. SHERRY looks behind the sofa.)*

SHERRY

Chance...!

> *(CHANCE pops up from behind the sofa in his pajamas and long nightcap, "wiping the sleep" from his eyes. FRANK can't believe it.)*

SHERRY
What were you doing back there?

CHANCE
I couldn't sleep.
> *(Looking at FRANK)*

What are you still doing here?

SHERRY
Now Chance, that's not nice. Apologize to Mister Johnson.

CHANCE
Sorry, Frank.

SHERRY
Now go to bed.

CHANCE
But Mama, I'm scared.
> *(Clutching her, terrified)*

The monsters might get me.

FRANK
> *(Aside)*

They should.

SHERRY

He's scared of the dark.

FRANK

(Aside)

That ain't all he should be scared of.

CHANCE

How was the movie, Mama?

SHERRY

Good, honey.

CHANCE

What did you guys see?

FRANK

(Aside)

Problem Child.

*(*SHERRY *shoots* FRANK *a look.)*

SHERRY

Frank... he's frightened? Look how he's holding me.

FRANK

He should be holding an Oscar.

SHERRY

I can't believe you're being so insensitive. He's a child, Frank, a kid.

FRANK

If you say so. Ya ask me, he's a forty-year-old midget with an attitude.

CHANCE

Mama, he called me a midget!

SHERRY

I think it's time for you to leave, Frank.

FRANK

Sherry, I was just kidding. I like Risk — Chance.

(FRANK *reaches for him, but*
CHANCE *won't let him touch
him.*)

CHANCE

You called me a midget.

FRANK
(To SHERRY*)*

It was a joke.

SHERRY

I'll let Chance make the call. Maybe if you say you're sorry
he'll let you stay.

(CHANCE *nods. It takes* FRANK
forever to say those two words.)

FRANK

I'm sorry. There. I said it.

CHANCE

I don't know if I'm ready to accept your apology yet. I'll have
to sleep on it. Can I get back to you?

(FRANK *looks at* SHERRY*, who
shrugs.*)

SHERRY
(Standing)

You heard what the man said.

                    FRANK
Sherry...

                    SHERRY
Goodnight, Frank.

                    (SHERRY leads him to the door.)

                    SHERRY
Like I said, I had a nice time.

                    FRANK
So did I until *Rosemary's Baby* showed up.

                    SHERRY
We'll have to do it again sometime.

                    FRANK
Sooner than later?

                    SHERRY
Set it up.

                    FRANK
You like amusement parks?

                    CHANCE
I do!

                    FRANK
So did *Bebe's Kids.*

                    SHERRY
Naa.

                    FRANK
How 'bout baseball?

                              SHERRY
Sometimes. Depends on who's playing.

                              FRANK
Dodgers and Giants Saturday afternoon.

                              SHERRY
Sounds like a plan.

                              FRANK
Get ready for Dodger dogs!

                              SHERRY
Can Chance come?

                              FRANK
Get back!
                    (Pleading)
I only have two tickets.

                              SHERRY
Can't we buy another one?

                              FRANK
We can, but we won't be sitting together. We'll be on the
third-base line, while *Doogie Howser* over there'll be in the
nose-bleed section which, the more I think about it, ain't such
a bad idea.

                              SHERRY
That wouldn't be right. We should all sit together.

                              FRANK
Can't you just take him another time, like after I'm dead?

                              CHANCE
No, I wanna come Saturday.

(FRANK *shoots him a wicked stare.* CHANCE *makes a funny face at him.* SHERRY *looks back at* CHANCE, *who's now staring at her innocently. She looks back at* FRANK.)

SHERRY

Let me think about it and call you. Maybe I can get my mother to take him to Chuck E Cheese or something.

CHANCE

I don't wanna go to Chuck E Cheese, I wanna see the Dodgers.

(FRANK *shoots him another look.* CHANCE *makes another funny face.*)

SHERRY
(*To* FRANK)

I'll call you.

(FRANK *nods and starts out.*)

SHERRY

Say goodnight to Mister Johnson, Chance.

CHANCE

Goodnight... Frank.

(FRANK *glares at him one last time [oh, if looks could kill] and exits.*)

(*Fade to black*)

END OF SCENE 4

<u>ACT I</u>

<u>Scene 5</u>

<u>SETTING</u>:   SHERRY*'s living room. Two days later.*

<u>AT RISE</u>:   *SFX: Phone rings five times.*

CHANCE enters, stage right, and answers it.

NOTE: FRANK should be in a spotlight, stage left, with a phone.

CHANCE

Hello.

FRANK

May I speak to your mother?

CHANCE

Who's calling?

FRANK

Frank.

CHANCE

Frank who?

FRANK

The Frank who's gonna come over there and kick ya little butt if you don't quit playin'!

(CHANCE hangs up. The telephone rings again.   CHANCE answers it.)

CHANCE
(Into phone)
Hello.

FRANK
(Into phone)
Man, why'd you hang up on me?!

CHANCE
You have an attitude.

FRANK
Put your mother on the phone — <u>now</u>.

CHANCE
Make me.

FRANK
You just wait 'til I talk to Sherry. You're gonna get your butt whipped, watch.

CHANCE
My mama doesn't whip me. I get punishment.

FRANK
You should get life, without the possibility of parole. Now would you go get your mother?

CHANCE
Say please.

FRANK
Look, punk! —

> *(CHANCE hangs up. The phone rings again. CHANCE answers it.)*

CHANCE
(Into phone)
Hello.

FRANK
(Into phone)
Please. Would you <u>please</u> put your mother on the phone?

CHANCE
Say pretty please... I'm'a hang up.

FRANK
Pretty please! Now put her on the phone!

CHANCE
With sugar on top?

FRANK
(Beat)
You know I'm gonna whip your ass, don't you?

(CHANCE hangs up. The tele-phone rings again. CHANCE answers it.)

CHANCE
(Into phone)
Hello.

FRANK
(Into phone)
With sugar on top. Anything else you want in my question, Rice Crispies, maybe?

CHANCE
Yeah, say that.

FRANK

Chance would you <u>please, pretty please, with sugar on top</u> and <u>Rice Crispies</u> in the middle, put your mother on the phone?

CHANCE

My mama ain't home!

> *(CHANCE hangs up, giggling, and exits. We fade out on the main set but keep the spotlight on FRANK.)*

FRANK
> *(Into phone)*

Hello... Hello!... Hello!!... Chance!... I'm gonna kill you, man! So say goodbye 'cause I don't care who you've got protecting you — your mama, your daddy, a pit bull, "The Terminator" — you're going down, man. Hear me?! You're going down!
> *(Beat)*

Damn, midget got me talking to myself.

> *(Black out.)*

END OF SCENE 5

ACT I

Scene 6

SETTING: SHERRY's *living room. Day.*

AT RISE: *It's Saturday afternoon. CHANCE is sitting on the sofa, wearing a complete baseball uniform, playing his video game. At his side is a baseball glove.*

SFX: A knock at the door.

CHANCE crosses to answer it. It's FRANK. CHANCE *smiles, a toothless grin.* FRANK *frowns, taking in* CHANCE's *appearance.*

FRANK

Where are you going?

CHANCE

To see the Dodgers.

FRANK
                    (Entering)
Not with me, you ain't.

CHANCE
                    (Following)
Yes, I am.

FRANK

No, you ain't.

CHANCE

Yes, I am.

FRANK

No, you ain't.

CHANCE

Yes, I am.

FRANK

You ain't!

CHANCE

I am!

FRANK

Ain't!

CHANCE

Am!

FRANK
(Realizing)
This is stupid! I'm arguing with a five-year-old.

CHANCE

I'm eight.

FRANK
Look, don't talk to me, okay?
(Sitting on the sofa)
Just pretend I'm not even here.

> *(CHANCE sits on the sofa next to
> him and resumes playing his video
> game.)*

FRANK
Where's your mother?
(Beat)
I said, where's your mother?

(Beat)
Look boy, I'm talking to you!

> *(CHANCE continues to play his video game. FRANK takes it from him. CHANCE tries to take it back, but FRANK struggles to keep it out of his reach.)*

CHANCE

Give me back my game!

FRANK

Not until you answer my question.

CHANCE

You told me to pretend you weren't here!

FRANK

Well, pretend I'm back.

CHANCE

My mother went to the store.

FRANK

The store? But she knew I was coming by at one o'clock.

CHANCE

She said she'd be right back.

> *(FRANK gives him back the game.)*

FRANK

Damn!

CHANCE

Don't be cussin' in my house.

(*FRANK shoots him a look.
CHANCE meets his stare then
resumes playing the video game.*)

FRANK

What time did she say she was coming back?

CHANCE
(*Shrugging*)
She just said she'll be back.

FRANK

Dang!
(*Off CHANCE's stare*)
I said "dang".

(*CHANCE resumes playing the
video game. He continually looks
at FRANK as he plays. FRANK
looks away. CHANCE keeps
dodging his stare. Finally,
CHANCE puts down the game and
picks up the glove. He sits back
and begins pounding his fist into
the pocket, an infielder anxious for
a ground ball. He pounds and
pounds and pounds and pounds,
gradually working FRANK's
nerves in the process. FRANK
grabs his glove and fist.*)

FRANK

Stop.

(*FRANK slowly, carefully releases
CHANCE's fist and glove. He sits
back again. CHANCE begins
pounding the glove again.
FRANK stares at him.*)

FRANK

Would you stop doing that?... <u>Please</u>.

(CHANCE stops.)

CHANCE

Where's your glove?

FRANK

I don't have one.

CHANCE

Tell your mama to buy you one.

FRANK

I don't need a glove.

CHANCE
                (Beat)
Want me to ask her?

FRANK

<u>I don't need a glove</u>.

CHANCE
                (Beat)
You scared of your mama, huh?

FRANK

No, I am not scared of my mama.

CHANCE

Then tell her to buy you a glove.

FRANK

I don't need a glove! Dang!
                (Off his look)
I said "dang."

CHANCE
(Pointing)
You're gonna get high blood pressure.

FRANK

What?

CHANCE

My mama said people who yell all the time get high blood pressure.

FRANK

What's high blood pressure?

CHANCE
(Shrugging)
I don't know.

(FRANK chuckles, hopelessly shaking his head.)

FRANK

I thought you were supposed to be going over to your father's house today.

CHANCE

I was, but he and my mama had an argument so he said he wouldn't come and get me.

FRANK
(Beat)
What were they arguing about?

CHANCE

None of your business.
(Pointing)
You're nosy.

FRANK

All right, you don't have to tell me.

CHANCE

They were arguing because my daddy said my mama should take me with her and my mama said, "No, I always take him with me. Why can't you watch him?" And my daddy said, "So. What about the money I sent you last week?" And my mama said, "What money?" And my daddy said —

FRANK

All right, I get it! I get it!

CHANCE

You asked.

FRANK
(Beat)
What does your father do?

CHANCE

Nothing.

FRANK

I mean, does he have a job?

CHANCE

Yeah.

FRANK

What does he do?

CHANCE
(Shrugging)
I don't know.

FRANK

It's all right. You don't have to tell me if you don't want to.
> *(Beat)*

I said you don't have to tell me if you don't want to.

CHANCE

Okay.

> *(FRANK leans back, defeated.*
> CHANCE *picks up his video*
> *game.)*

CHANCE

My mama calls him a street pharmacist, but every time I ask
her what that is she won't tell me.

FRANK

> *(Beat)*

Do you like your father?

CHANCE

No.

FRANK

How come?
> *(Beat)*

How come you don't like your father?

CHANCE

> *(Looking away)*

'Cause he's always hitting my mama.
> *(Beat)*

That's why he don't live with us no more.

> *(FRANK looks at him with new-*
> *found eyes.)*

FRANK
                    (Carefully)
Is that why you don't want anybody going out with your
mama?

                              (CHANCE *nods. FRANK moves*
                              closer to him. Puts an arm around
                              his shoulder.)

                    FRANK
I don't want to hurt your mama. I like your mama.

                    CHANCE
Yeah, yeah, that's what they all say.

                    FRANK
Chance, I would <u>never</u> hit your mother.

                    CHANCE
                    (Beat)
Never?

                    FRANK
<u>Never</u>.

                    CHANCE
                    (Beat)
You promise?

                    FRANK
I promise.

                    CHANCE
                    (Beat)
Swear to God?

                    FRANK
            (Scout's honor)
I swear to God!

                    CHANCE
It's not good to swear.

                    FRANK
C'mere.

                            (FRANK gives him a warm hug.
                            CHANCE returns the affection.
                            FRANK looks at his watch.)

                    CHANCE
My mama's gonna make us miss the game, huh?

                            (FRANK looks at him for a beat,
                            then shakes his head.)

                    FRANK
No.
            (Standing)
Let's go.

                    CHANCE
To the game?
            (Off his nod)
But what about my mama?

                            (FRANK thinks for a beat, pulls
                            out the two tickets and tosses them
                            on the center table.   CHANCE
                            grins from here to Yankee Stadium,
                            grabs his glove and stands.
                            FRANK starts for the door,
                            CHANCE in tow.)

                    CHANCE
Where are we sittin', Mister Johnson?

                    FRANK
In the nose-bleed section. And please, call me Frank.

                    CHANCE
All right... Frank.

                    (CHANCE *grabs his hand. They
                    continue for the door, hand-in-
                    hand, a father and son embarking
                    on an outing.*)

                    CHANCE
What's the nose-bleed section?

                    FRANK
The seats way up top, in the upper deck.

                    CHANCE
But we won't be able to see the game!

                    FRANK
Yes, we will.

                    CHANCE
No, we won't.

                    FRANK
We will!

                    CHANCE
We won't!

FRANK

Will!

CHANCE

Won't!

*(*FRANK *and* CHANCE *exit and we:)*

(Black out.)

END OF SCENE 6

ACT I

Scene 7

SETTING: SHERRY's *living room. Night.*

AT RISE: SHERRY *is on the phone.   She looks disheveled, if not a tad frantic.*

SHERRY
(Into phone)
Yes Mama, I called his daddy. He's looking too.
(Beat)
Yes Mama, I called the police.
(Beat)
No Mama, I haven't called *Cops* yet. But if he doesn't turn up in the next hour I just might.

*(*FRANK *and* CHANCE *enter.)*

SHERRY
(Into phone)
He just walked in. I'll call you later, Mama.
(Hangs up, to CHANCE*)*
Where have you been?!

CHANCE
We went to see the Dodger game.

*(*SHERRY *stares at* FRANK.*)*

SHERRY
How could you take my child out of this house without even leaving me so much as a note? Do you know how worried I was?

FRANK

You didn't see the tickets I left for you?

SHERRY

That's your idea of a note? Two lousy tickets to a baseball game?

FRANK

Those were not lousy tickets. They were box seats on the third-base line.

SHERRY

I don't give a rat's ass if they were in the dugout.

FRANK

Yeah, well, for your information they cost me fifty bucks.

SHERRY

What's fifty bucks for "the woman of your dreams"?

FRANK

(Beat)

Fifty dollars.

CHANCE

You guys are gonna get high blood pressure.

> *(SHERRY and FRANK look at CHANCE. SHERRY pulls CHANCE near and holds him dearly.)*

SHERRY

I thought someone had kidnapped my baby.

FRANK

Look, Sherry, I'm sorry.

                              CHANCE
Mama, look.

                    (CHANCE *opens the glove to*
                    reveal a scuffed baseball.)

                              SHERRY
You caught a foul ball?

                              CHANCE
No, Frank did. He gave it to me.

                    (SHERRY *pulls* FRANK *aside.)*

                              SHERRY
How come you guys left me?

                              FRANK
We waited for you as long as we could.

                              SHERRY
I just went to the store.

                              FRANK
Where, in Mississippi?

                              CHANCE
Yeah, Mama, you were taking all day. We had to roll.

                              SHERRY
Be quiet!

                              FRANK
That wasn't nice.

                              SHERRY
Shut up, Frank.

CHANCE

Don't tell him to shut up.
(Taking FRANK's hand)
He's my friend.

SHERRY

Your friend?
(Off his nod)
I thought you couldn't stand him?

(FRANK reacts.)

CHANCE

I changed my mind.

SHERRY

Did he give you some money?

(CHANCE nods.)

SHERRY

I knew it! Where's the money he gave you?

CHANCE

In my tummy. I used it to buy a Dodger dog.

(SHERRY pulls FRANK aside.)

SHERRY

What did you do to him?

FRANK

Do to him?

SHERRY

Yes. He hates every man I date.

FRANK

Maybe you're finally dating the <u>right</u> man.

(SHERRY shoots FRANK a look.)

CHANCE

You guys need to talk.

(CHANCE starts for his bed-room.)

SHERRY

Where are you going?

CHANCE

To relax. I've had a long day.
          (Beat)
We still going to the zoo next week, Frank?

FRANK

Nine o'clock next Saturday.

CHANCE

Make it ten. That way, I won't miss my cartoons.

FRANK

You're the man.

CHANCE

No, you're the man.

FRANK

No, you're the man.

CHANCE

No, you're —

SHERRY

— Frank!

(FRANK *reacts.* CHANCE *yawns.*)

CHANCE

Goodnight, Frank.

FRANK

Goodnight, Chance.

(CHANCE *exits.* SHERRY *looks at* FRANK, *sheepishly.*)

SHERRY

Can I go?

(FRANK *begins pacing the room.*)

FRANK

Uh, I don't know. I'll have to sleep on it. Can I get back to you?

(SHERRY *gives him a kiss.*)

FRANK

Okay.

(FRANK *kisses her again and they hug. As* FRANK *throws us a big wink:*)

(*Black out.*)

THE END

THE RIDE

ACT I

Scene 1

SETTING #1:   *Darkness. We hear a montage of news footage.*

NEWSMAN #1 (V.O.)

The two victims died of sharp, forced injuries and multiple stab wounds.

NEWSMAN #2 (V.O.)

Simpson was briefly handcuffed at home then driven to police headquarters for about three hours of questioning.

ROBERT SHAPIRO (V.O.)

He has spent the night with his two young children and with his family. He is extremely depressed. He is under the care of a physician to help him through this very difficult time of grief.

NEWSMAN #2 (V.O.)

Investigators refuse to say Simpson is a suspect.

NEWSWOMAN #1 (V.O.)

Two funerals today for two victims. In Westlake, a service for Ronald Goldman — the young man killed in the attack. And in Brentwood, a service for Nicole Simpson. Her ex-husband, O.J. Simpson, was there.

PETER JENNINGS (V.O.)

In Los Angeles this afternoon, the great football legend was charged with murdering his former wife and a friend.

POLICE SPOKESMAN (V.O.)
Mister Simpson, in agreement with his attorney, was scheduled to surrender this morning to the Los Angeles Police Department. Initially, that was eleven o'clock. It then became eleven forty-five. Mister Simpson has not appeared.

GIL GARCETTI (V.O.)
Mister Simpson is a fugitive right now. And if you assist him, in any way, you are committing a felony.

911 OPERATOR (V.O.)
This is nine-one-one. What are you reporting?

AL COWLINGS (V.O.)
This is A.C. I have O.J. in the car.

911 OPERATOR (V.O.)
Okay. Where are you?

AL COWLINGS (V.O.)
Please. I'm coming up the Five freeway.

911 OPERATOR (V.O.)
Okay.

AL COWLINGS (V.O.)
Right now, we're okay. But ya gotta tell the police just to back off. He's still alive, but he's got a gun to his head.

(Black out.)

<u>END OF SCENE 1</u>

Act I

Scene 2

SETTING #2: *It is late afternoon on June 17, 1994. We are in* AL COWLINGS' *white Ford Bronco, which is slowly moving along the 405 Freeway, being cautiously pursued by a team of police cars. Police and news helicopters also litter the sky above. On either side of the freeway, dozens of cars are parked and motorists are standing beside their vehicles watching the slow-speed chase in disbelief.*

AT RISE: *Seated behind the wheel of the Bronco is a stone-faced* AL COWLINGS. *He closes the flip phone he's holding and puts it in the passenger seat. But the real shocker is in the back seat —* O.J. SIMPSON. *He's slumped over, holding a gun to his head and wearing a bad disguise. Even with the phony beard and mustache, dark glasses and fedora,* O.J. *looks distraught.*

A.C.

How much longer do you wanna keep doing this O.J.?

O.J.

Just keep driving.

                    A.C.
O.J., the tank is half empty.

                    O.J.
I like to think of it as half full.

                    A.C.
You can think whatever you want. In a half hour, we're gonna
be out of gas.

                    O.J.
Then let's worry about that in a half hour, okay?

                    (A.C. looks back at him.)

                    A.C.
O.J., you look ridiculous. Why don't you take off that disguise? Everybody knows you're in here.

                    O.J.
Just keep driving, all right?

                    *(A.C. shakes his head and keeps
                    driving. O.J. slowly takes off the
                    fake beard, mustache, shades and
                    hat. A.C. looks in the rearview.)*

                    A.C.
What about all of those police cars behind us? How much
longer you think they're gonna put up with this shit?

                    O.J.
They're gonna put up with it as long as my name is O.J.
Simpson.

                    A.C.
O.J. Simpson is not above the law.

O.J.

O.J. Simpson is a celebrity, a superstar.

A.C.

O.J. Simpson is a Black man, a brother... a nigga. You lucky they ain't shot us yet.

(O.J. peeks out of the window.)

O.J.

Look at all those people out there, A.C. Look at 'em. Lining up and down the freeway, waving signs: "Go O.J.," "Don't Squeeze The Juice." Those are my fans. The police aren't gonna do anything to me as long as they're out here. If the police shoot me, the whole city will burn.

A.C.

You shouldn't believe your own press, O.J.

O.J.

I didn't make it up. Everybody knows it's true. Whites, Blacks, Latinos, Asians — everybody will riot, because you cannot take the life of a legend. Only a legend can take down a legend.

A.C.

Oh, so Elvis and Bruce Lee can shoot you but the L.A.P.D. can't?

O.J.

That's not what I meant, and you know it. Besides, Elvis and Bruce Lee ain't dead. They're just in seclusion somewhere.

A.C.

Look man, if you're gonna believe your own press then you've gotta believe what they're saying right now — that you killed Nicole.

O.J.
(Waving the gun at A.C.*)*
I did not kill Nicole and you know it!

A.C.
Hey, look man, don't point that gun at me. You wanna blow your own brains out, be my guest. But I ain't going with you.

O.J.
Then why are you here?

A.C.
I've been asking myself that all afternoon.

(O.J. sits back, composed.)

O.J.
A.C., I would never hurt Nicole. You know that. <u>You know that</u>.

A.C.
All I know is what you told me, man. You're my boy so I believe you. But what about what the police say? They got blood, they found a glove. I mean, it doesn't look good, O.J.

O.J.
They're trying to set me up, man. They're trying to set me up!

A.C.
Why? If they're trying to set you up, <u>why</u> are they trying to set you up, O.J.?

O.J.
'Cause I'm a rich Black man who likes blonde White women.

A.C.
I'm a Black man. I like blonde White women. How come they're not trying to set me up?

O.J.

You ain't rich. They don't see your face on TV every day. You ain't in commercials, jumping over suitcases in the airport. You ain't making movies. You're not one of the best running backs of all-time. You're not a threat, man. I am a threat.

(Pause)

You know how it is when a brother has power. When a brother has a little money. They don't like that shit. So they gotta squelch it, man. They gotta put you in your place.

A.C.

I thought you weren't a brother? I thought you were a "celebrity"... a "superstar"?

O.J.

I'm not stupid, A.C. I am a celebrity. I am a superstar. But I'll always be Black in their eyes first. <u>Always</u>.

A.C.

I don't know. The shit just don't make sense, O.J.

O.J.

Did Rodney King make sense? Did Ron Settles make sense? Did Yula Love make sense? Did Emmett Till make sense?

A.C.

Oh, so now you're a martyr in the struggle. Brother, when was the last time you've been to the 'hood?

O.J.

The 'hood ain't got nothing to do with this!

A.C.

Then neither should being Black.

(O.J. hopelessly shakes his head.)

O.J.

You sound like a white boy, A.C.

A.C.

I sound like a white boy? You've been living like one for the last twenty-five years!

O.J.

(Waving the gun at A.C.)

Stop judging me, man.

A.C.

Don't point that gun at me, O.J.! I told you!

O.J.

You know me, A.C. You know I ain't no sellout, especially after all I've done for you.

A.C.

You mean, like... steal my girl?

O.J.

C'mon man, we were in high school.

A.C.

She was still my girl, O.J. Marguerite was <u>my</u> woman. You knew that but you took her anyway. And then you married her.

(Pause.)

O.J.

Man, am I going to spend the rest of my life apologizing to you for that? C'mon, A.C., we were kids. I was stupid, man.

(Pause)

You make it sound like I haven't looked out for you, man. Okay, I took your first love. I took your high school sweet heart. But I also took you with me. When all those coaches all over the country were saying, "We want The Juice," and I chose SC, I said, "I ain't going unless you take my boy, my best friend — A.C." C'mon, man. And then when I left SC and I went to Buffalo, who came with me? I said, "If yawl want me as your top pick, you've got to take my boy A.C. too." When I got traded to 'Frisco, who did I bring with me? — You. When I did that HBO series, *First and Ten*, who did I help get a part on the show? — You.

A.C.

You never got me on *Naked Gun*.

O.J.

(Pause)
All my life, I've looked out for you, A.C.

A.C.

Man, I look out for you too. You think I'd just let anybody use my Bronco for a slow-speed chase on the Four-oh-five?

(O.J. looks away.)

O.J.

Who bought you this Bronco, A.C.?

A.C.

I knew that was coming. I knew it!
(Taking a deep breath)
You know O.J., sometimes I think the only reason why you bought me this Bronco is so I could spend the rest of my life thanking you for it.

O.J.

See, that's my problem. I'm too generous. Marguerite always told me I was too giving. So did Nicole.

A.C.

Who... who do you think did it, O.J.?

O.J.
(Uncomfortable pause)

I don't know.

A.C.

Kato?

O.J.

Kato?... Kato? No way. Kato doesn't even know how to pay rent.

A.C.
(Carefully)

Jason?

(O.J.'s face registers horror.)

O.J.

Don't you dare... How dare you say that, A.C.?!

A.C.

Hey man, I love Jason! I'm not accusing him of anything. But they're whispering things. And one of the things they're whispering is that Jason didn't like Nicole. And you know how the media is. They'll take two and two and somehow get five.
(Pause)

I'm just asking a question.

O.J.

Well, I don't appreciate that question, man! Jason is my son!

A.C.

He's my godson. You think I believe he could ever do something like that?

O.J.

Then why would you even go there?
(Pause)
All right, Jason wasn't crazy about Nicole. Would he kill her?
No. Hell no! Never. Never, A.C. Jason is a good boy.

A.C.

(Confused)
Then how... how did that blood get in the house, O.J.?

O.J.

... I don't know... I told you, it's... it's a set-up.

A.C.

The media... the media thinks you did it.

O.J.

I don't care what the media thinks. If I had listened to the
media I would've never got out of the projects and gone to college; if I had listened to the media, every time I had a bad
game I should've hung up my cleats and went to work for the
post office; if I had listened to the media I would've never
done those Hertz commercials because America wasn't ready
for a Black face to tell it where to rent cars; if I had listened to
the media I'd be in prison, on parole or on probation; if I had
listened to the media, A.C., I wouldn't be nothing. So the
media can kiss my Black ass because I am absolutely, one hundred percent, not guilty.

(Long pause.)

A.C.

If you're "absolutely, one hundred percent not guilty" like you
say, prove it in court.

O.J.

In court? Look behind us: there're thirty-something police cars back there. There're so many helicopters up in the sky I'm surprised one of them ain't crashed yet. Look at all those people lining the freeway; standing on the overpass. I mean, people have actually parked their cars, gotten out, and are standing on their hoods, watching <u>us</u>, A.C. That's my potential jury. Whether they're for me or against me, they've all been contaminated by this... this madness. A trial would only take this... this public feeding frenzy to another level. And quite frankly, A.C., I don't know if I wanna put my family through this. I mean, you know they'll take everything I've got. Everything I've worked for my whole life will go right into the hands of the legal system, whether I'm found innocent or guilty. And I'll be right back where I started... where <u>we</u> started, A.C. — with nothing.

A.C.
                    (Pause)
Maybe.

O.J.

I can't do that to my kids, A.C. I've worked too hard, man. It's not fair — to them or me.

A.C.

Oh, but blowing your brains out, in front of the whole world, is? That'll make 'em real proud of you, O.J.

O.J.

Shut up!

A.C.

The only way you're gonna shut me up is if you aim that gun at me and pull the trigger.
                    (Pause)
I'm in this too, you know. You ever think about that? What's gonna happen to A.C.?

O.J.

C'mon man, you're not being accused of murder.

A.C.

Last time I checked, harboring a fugitive was a federal offense. I am risking my life for you, brother. And you're gonna tell me to shut up? Uh-uh, I'm gonna talk. I've earned that right.

O.J.

I don't have to listen to you—

A.C.

I've been listening to you all week! "A.C., I'm innocent;" "A.C., I've been set up," "A.C., they're trying to get me." Have I ever told you to shut up?

O.J.

Oh, so what'chu trying to say now... that I'm boring you with my problems? Is that it?
(Pause)
Pull over and get out. Go. I can take over from here.

A.C.

O.J., you cannot hold a gun to your head and drive at the same time.

O.J.

What'chu talking about, man? It's just like running and carrying a football. In fact, running with a football is harder because you got people trying to tackle you. All I got to worry about is the road — a speed bump here or there.

A.C.

There's a big difference, man: football is a game; this is real life. In real life, you can't run every time you see trouble coming. Sometimes you have to stand there and take the hit.

O.J.
(Pause)

It's funny. I've spent my whole life trying not to become a statistic; a stereotype of what a brother is supposed to be. Went to college. Played pro ball. Saved my money. Had a family. Worked in broadcasting. Made movies. I was a role model, man, to millions of kids — Black <u>and</u> white — all over the world. Now look at me. I'm in the very place I swore I'd never be. It's almost like, what was the point of doing all those wonderful things with my life if all I'd become in the end...

A.C.

It's not too late to turn yourself in, O.J.

O.J.

If I turn myself in, A.C., I'm dead.

A.C.

I don't think they'd ask for the death penalty.

O.J.

I'm not talking about the death penalty. I told you, you can't kill a legend. You think if Frank Sinatra killed somebody he'd get the death penalty? He wouldn't even go to jail. He'd get probation. Or a suspended sentence. Or an acquittal. And nobody would say nothing. They'd say, "Hey, he's Frank Sinatra. What do you want us to do, lock him up? He's a musical genius, an icon, a legend. And everyone knows you can't kill a legend."

A.C.

I hate to be the one to tell you this, O.J., but you're not Frank Sinatra.

O.J.

Legends come in all shapes, sizes and colors. He's a musical legend; I'm a sports legend. A legend, is a legend, is a legend.

A.C.

C'mon O.J., Frank Sinatra... he's bigger than life, man. He's...
he's —

O.J.

A legend! Just like me! You just forget because we're friends.
To you, I'm just O.J. But to the world, I'm "The Juice." I'm
a legend.

A.C.

Are all "legends" full of themselves?

O.J.

Why are we even talking about the death penalty? Hell, I'm
innocent.

A.C.

Then turn yourself in.

O.J.

I told you, if I turn myself in I'm dead.

A.C.

C'mon, O.J., dead?

O.J.

Not physically, socially. It's called character assassination,
and it started the day of the murders. The press made me a
suspect; the next day they charged me; I was convicted the day
after that, and I still hadn't been officially charged with anything. The media chipped away at what used to be my good
name, like a pack of vultures picking at a wounded carcass. If
they pick at it long enough they'll kill it. There's no way my
hide can survive a trial that may take months... maybe even a
year. By the time it's all over, there'll be nothing left of O.J.
Simpson. Even if I'm found innocent, when have you ever
known the press to apologize?

(Pause)

Did they apologize to the McMartin family after those child molestation charges turned out to be false? "MEDIA APOLO-GIZES TO McMARTINS"? Ever see that in the paper? Hell no! But for ten years, they fed off of their tragedy, their pain, to sell their stupid newspapers.
(Pause)
When you hear the word McMartin, what do you think of? Child molestation. When they're through with me, O.J. Simpson will stand for wife killer. So you see, A.C., O.J. Simpson is a dead man, waiting to be buried.
(Brandishing the gun)
I may as well pull the trigger and do myself a favor.

A.C.

I can't believe you, O.J.

O.J.

You think I'm weak.

A.C.

No, I think you're selfish. I mean, you got four kids. What's gonna happen to them after you blow your brains out?

O.J.

Arnelle and Jason are grown.

A.C.

Oh, they're grown. So I guess that means they don't need their daddy no more.

O.J.

They'll understand.

A.C.

What about Sidney and Justin? Will they understand?
(Pause)

They've already lost their mama, O.J. Now their daddy's gonna "do them a favor" and take himself out. How do you think that's gonna affect them? I mean, who's gonna take care of them, man? Who's gonna take them to Little League and ballet? Who's gonna help them with their homework? Who's gonna be there to see them graduate from high school? Who man? Me? I mean, I'm'a do what I can but I'm not their daddy so it ain't gonna be the same.

(Pause)

If you do this, man, your children are gonna spend the rest of their lives trying to cope with the fact that when they needed their daddy most, he abandoned them.

O.J.

I'm not abandoning them!

A.C.

You are! You're running because you're scared but it's wrong, man! It's selfish and it's wrong!

O.J.

What else can I do, A.C.? <u>What else can I do</u>?

A.C.

All I know is, suicide is not the answer. If anything, it just makes you look more guilty.

O.J.

I just want the pain to end, A.C.

A.C.

I know you do, man, I know you do. And it will. But not like this. Not with a gun, man. The only way you can prove your innocence is in court.

O.J.

I won't get a fair trial!

A.C.

You'll get the best trial your money can buy, which is more
than I can say for most brothers in your situation. Most brothers wouldn't have a chance in hell of seeing justice. You do.

O.J.

What about the court of public opinion? Just because I don't
go to jail doesn't mean I'll be free, A.C. The only way I can
get my name back is to find the people who killed Nicole, and
I'm not a private investigator.

A.C.

Hire one. Hell, hire two.

O.J.

This whole thing is like a nightmare. Only it's on <u>my</u> street...
in my mind.
                    (Fighting back tears)
I want the nightmare to stop! I just want it to stop!

A.C.

O.J., if you pull that trigger you're gonna mess up my car,
man. Now, I know you bought it, but you gave it to me so it's
mine, and I don't want your brains all over it.

O.J.

The price you pay for aiding and abetting an arthritic, knock-
kneed, suicidal fugitive, who also happens to be —

O.J./A.C.

A legend.

                    (A.C. shoots him a knowing look.
                    O.J. smiles for the first time.)

A.C.

You ever think about what's gonna happen to your soul after
you pull the trigger?

                    O.J.
I'll be dead.

                    A.C.
After that.

                    O.J.
          (Considering)
I'll be buried, or cremated... depending on how bad I look. I'll
let you decide—

                    A.C.
— I'm talking about your soul, O.J.

                    O.J.
My soul will be in heaven, with God.

                         (A.C. *pulls a Bible from under his*
                         seat.)

                    A.C.
But the Bible says that suicide is a sin.

                         (A.C. *hands* O.J. *the Bible.)*

                    O.J.
The Bible also says it's a sin to lie, cheat, steal and carouse.
But everybody does it and God knows everybody does it
because God understands. We're human. And as long as
we're human we're gonna make mistakes.

                    A.C.
What Bible you been reading?

                              O.J.
It's in there.
                    (Handing A.C. back the Bible)
Look it up. Maybe not word for word, but I'm giving you the
basic rundown.

                              A.C.
In the Bible, God says that if you destroy your temple, it auto-
matically qualifies you for a front row seat in hell.
                    (Handing O.J. the Bible)
It's in there. Look it up.

                              O.J.
                    (Handing Bible back to A.C.)
God makes exceptions.

                              A.C.
No, He doesn't. Not even for legends. In fact, historically
He's been harder on legends. Ya ask me, I think it's because
He figures yawl've been spoiled rotten all the while yawl were
on earth.
                    (Pause)
So however you slice it, if you take your own life you're going
to hell.

                              O.J.
You're just trying to scare me.

                              A.C.
It's in the book. Look it up.

                              *(A.C. tries to hand the Bible to
                              O.J. but he won't take it.)*

                              O.J.

I don't feel like reading right now.

A.C.

'Cause you know I'm right.

O.J.

Why don't you turn on some music? Wait a minute, isn't the game on? Yeah, Houston's playing New York. Turn it on, A.C.

A.C.

Turn what on, man? I don't have a TV in here. This ain't a limo.

O.J.

Game's probably over anyway.

A.C.

Stop kidding yourself, man. You know nobody's watching that basketball game. This is the only show in town.

O.J.

I can't go to jail, A.C. And I sure as hell can't go to hell. That means...
(Handing A.C. the gun)
...you gotta do it for me, A.C.

A.C.

Uh-uh! I ain't going to hell either. Not for you, not for my mama, not for nobody. I'll take a bullet for you, but I won't put one in you. So if you're gonna pull that trigger you better hurry up 'cause we're about on "E" and I think every cop in L.A. is behind us.

O.J.

I can't, man!

A.C.

What do you mean? A second ago, you were ready to paint my van red.

                           O.J.

That's before you told me that damn Bible story. Now I've lost my nerve.

                           A.C.

You don't wanna go to jail; you don't wanna go to hell; you don't wanna go to trial; you don't wanna pull over. We almost out of gas, O.J. What'chu wanna do?

                           O.J.
                (Pausing to consider)
I wanna go back to Rockingham.

                           A.C.

Rockingham? What'chu wanna do there?

                           O.J.

First of all, I gotta take a leak. After I do that, I'm'a need something to drink — preferably a glass of O.J. Then I wanna call my mother and tell her that... I'm gonna turn myself in.

                          (A.C. smiles, relieved, then hands him the cell phone.)

                           A.C.

You can call her right now, on the cell.

                           O.J.

The reception is better from Rockingham.

                          (O.J. sits back.)

                           A.C.
              (Putting down the phone)
You're the legend.

                           O.J.

And you're the best friend a legend ever had, A.C.

(A.C. puts out his hand, expectant-
ly. O.J. looks at it for a beat then
slowly hands over the gun. A.C.
puts it under the seat.)

A.C.

Next stop — Rockingham.

(Black out.)

VOICE OVER

(Over black out)

On October third, Nineteen Ninety-Five at ten-oh-nine a.m. —
four hundred and seventy-four days after being charged with
the brutal slayings of Nicole Brown Simpson and Ronald
Goldman — a jury of nine Blacks, two Whites and one Latino
found Orenthal James Simpson not guilty of first-degree murder. At eleven-sixteen, on the same day, Simpson was taken to
his Brentwood estate, by police escort, in a white minivan. As
he exited the van in the courtyard of his home, the first person
to greet him, with a hearty bear hug, was Al Cowlings.

THE END

HAPPY ANNIVERSARY, PUNK!

ACT I

Scene 1

SETTING: AL BEAN-FLETCHER'S *living room. It is mid-afternoon.*

AT RISE: AL BEAN-FLETCHER, *40, is center stage. He's in street clothes. A bottle of liquor sits at his feet. [NOTE: During his monologue he will change to his postal uniform.])*

AL

One hundred million, eight hundred-forty thousand seconds. One million, nine hundred-fourteen thousand minutes. Twenty-one thousand, nine hundred hours. Three hundred sixty-five days. Fifty-two weeks. Twelve months. Damn! I can't believe it's been a year.

(Beat)

I remember it like yesterday. I was at the post office, having my annual review. The phone rings. I assume it's my wife, calling to find out if I got that promotion. I'm right. It's her.

(Beat)

Our son had been shot on his way home from school. She was at the hospital. By the time I got there, he was gone.

(Beat)

Randall. Randall Bean-Fletcher. I wanted to name him Al, after me. But making a boy go through life being called by another man's name just didn't seem right to me. Sure, I had to do it. But I didn't have a choice. What can a newborn say when his daddy names him "Junior"? "Feed me!" So when I became a daddy I decided to play God and change the rules.

(Beat)

Most fathers would spend a day like this at the cemetery or picketing in front of the courthouse, demanding a retrial. My wife's at the cemetery right now with her mother. Not me. Cemeteries are like all other rituals of death — they're for the living. The dead don't care. Hell, they're dead. Besides, I'm tired of crying. Nope. Ain't gonna be no more tears coming out of these eyes. No, sir! I'm a man, goddamnit! Leave the whimpering and whining to the women and children. Real men don't cry — they get even.

    (Beat)

The kid who killed Randall was a year older than him. Only fifteen years old. They caught him, locked him up for nine months, then let him out. Said he was no longer a "danger to society." Said he was "reformed." Sometimes, when I'm watering the lawn, I see him drive by my house in his mama's Honda, seat cocked back pimp-daddy style, lookin' like Snoop Hot Diggity Damn Dog. He don't say nothin', but I can hear him loud and clear: "I'm <u>free</u>! I'm <u>free</u>! And ain't nothin' you can do to <u>me</u>, old <u>dude</u>. Be <u>cool</u>."

    (Beat)

Kids can be so stupid. They think just because you're grown you gotta be responsible all the time, do the right thing; that you can't just nut up and go crazy, like them. Well, today, I'm pleading "temporary insanity".

    (AL exits as we:)

    (Black out.)

<u>END OF SCENE 1</u>

ACT I

Scene 2

SETTING: *The living room of* SHAWN "BIG MAC" WILLIAMS. *Sparse but very tasteful. There's a leather sofa, smoked-glass center table with a Tina Allen sculpture atop it, Persian rug, state-of-the-art stereo system adjacent an antique chair. A portrait of a black Jesus over- looks the sofa. The front door is stage left, there's a hallway upstage and a window stage right.*

AT RISE: *Same day.   Thirty minutes later.* SHAWN   "BIG   MAC" WILLIAMS *is lying on the sofa, talking on a cordless telephone. Rap music is playing on his nearby boom box.*

BIG MAC
(Into phone)
C'mon, baby, you gon' give me a little kitty cat or what?... I gotta beg for it?! Girl, you must be on crack. Big Mac don't beg for jack... in the box!
(Laughs at his own joke)
Okay, but only for you. Only for my... kitty cat: "Meow! Meow! Meow! Meow, Meow, Meow!" How was that?... Hello?
(Hangs up)
Trick! That's why she ain't got no boyfriend.
(Dials again, puts phone to his ear)
Can I speak to Raleethia?... What?!... No *habla* English? Well, what can you *habla?*...

(Hangs up)

Can't believe that bitch gave me the wrong number. That's why she ain't got no boyfriend.

(Dials again, putting phone to his ear)

Hello, Shaquita? This is Mac... <u>Mac</u>... I met you in detention on the last day of school?... Right, right. The brother who was sagging with no drawers on. Hell yeah, all that booty was mine —

> *(AL enters through the window like a prowler, unbeknownst to BIG MAC. When he finally sees AL, he bolts from the sofa..)*

BIG MAC

(Urgently, into phone)

Shaquita, call — !

(As AL points the gun at him)

... me back.

(Hangs up; to AL)

Hi.

AL

Sit down and shut up.

BIG MAC

What's up?

AL

I said, sit down and shut up.

> *(BIG MAC crosses back to the sofa and sits. AL shuts the window and begins casing the room to make sure no one else is around.)*

BIG MAC
Yo, don't I know you?

(AL ignores him, pulls over a chair and sits across from him, keeping his gun on BIG MAC the whole time.)

BIG MAC
You're homeboy's popz, huh?

(AL stares at him.)

AL
Do you know what "shut up" means?

BIG MAC
Yo man, I didn't kill your son, it was an accident.

AL
(Hitting him with the gun butt)
I said, shut up!
(Beat)
Now, I don't wanna hear that shit. I heard it in court for two weeks. An accident my black ass! My son didn't do <u>nothin'</u> to you. Nothin'! He was a good kid. <u>A good kid!</u> He didn't deserve to die in the street like a dog. And you... you put him there.

BIG MAC
I —

AL
(Putting the gun to his neck)
— said, shut up! Don't say a damn thing. Did you let Randall say anything before you took his breath away forever? Did you?! Huh? Did you, you worthless piece of shit?!

> *(AL wants to squeeze the trigger but doesn't. Instead, he regains his composure and retreats to the chair, still pointing the gun.)*

                    BIG MAC

I—

                    AL

You talk when I tell you to talk.

> *(BIG MAC raises his hand. AL nods like a schoolteacher.)*

                    BIG MAC

Can I talk?

                    AL

<u>May</u> I speak.

                    BIG MAC

<u>May</u> I speak?

                    AL

No. You just sit there and keep looking into the barrel of this pistol and imagine what it's gonna feel like when I pull the trigger and a bullet the size of a roach comes out so fast you won't even see it blow your heart apart like a grenade. All the blood in your body is gonna come gushing out like a busted fire hydrant until there's no more life left in your skinny, sorry ass.

                    BIG MAC

Why you wanna —

                    AL

Did I say you could talk?!

(*BIG MAC raises his hand. AL nods.*)

BIG MAC

Why you wanna shoot me in the heart? Why don't you just shoot me in the head and get it over with?

AL

Because I want you to suffer, just like Randall did before he went. I wanna see you suffer, like my wife and I have been suffering. I want you to feel our pain, and your mama's pain for making the mistake of bringing you into this world. I'm destroying your heart because you don't need one.

BIG MAC

Yo, can we leave my mama out of this?

AL

Why? Didn't she start this whole mess? I'm sure if she knew she was carrying "Damien" she would've had an abortion.

(*BIG MAC starts for him. AL cocks the gun. BIG MAC stops.*)

AL

Come on! Give me a reason to say "accident."

(*BIG MAC sits down. With his gun aimed at BIG MAC, AL pulls the liquor bottle out of his pocket and takes a swig.*)

AL

Your mother's probably a nice lady. I bet she wishes you were never born too. She's probably out there working a double

shift so she doesn't have to come home and see the sad little
bastard she thought was a blessing but is nothing more than a
curse.

                    BIG MAC
Shut up.

                    AL
If I take your life, will your mama miss you?

                    BIG MAC
Shut up.

                    AL
Will she thank me?

                    BIG MAC
Shut up!

                    AL
Shake my hand?

                    BIG MAC
Shut up!

                    AL
Give me a reward?

                    BIG MAC
Shut up!!

                    AL
Cash?

                    BIG MAC
Shut up!!

> AL
>> *(Like an announcer)*

"A new car!"

>> *(*BIG MAC *covers his ears and hums.)*

> AL

Yeah, your mama'll be so happy she don't have to deal with your ass no more, she'll be dancing like Josephine Baker.

>> *(*BIG MAC *stops covering his ears.)*

> BIG MAC

It's a good thing you got that gun, 'cause if I had it I'd —

> AL

You'd what?
>> *(Standing over him)*

What?! Pull the trigger? Come on, Quarter Pounder, tell me what I should do. Should I pull the trigger the way you pulled it for my son? Should I, you filthy sewer rat!
>> *(Putting the barrel in* AL's *mouth)*

What's the matter, you don't like the Happy Meal I got you?

>> *(*BIG MAC *is gagging violently now.* AL *finally relents and pushes him back on the sofa.* BIG MAC *begins gasping for air. He falls to the ground, still panting and puffing, and begins to crawl.)*

> AL
>> *(Leading him back to sofa by his collar)*

Where ya goin', Small Fry? I still wanna play.

BIG MAC
Man, why don't you just shoot me.

AL
I told you. I want you to suffer. You're going out like a bottle of Heinz ketchup — real slow.

BIG MAC
You're sick!

AL
No, I'm what they call a "conversation piece." They study people like me. Write books. Make movies. Put us on talk shows.
            (Beat)
People like you, they throw rocks at, spit on, fry. It's shake 'n bake, baby. And when that doesn't work — and, in this case, it didn't — there's only one solution, and I'm holding it right here.
            (Pointing the gun at him)
Get on your knees. I wanna see you beg.
            (No response)
I said get on your knees, punk!
            (As BIG MAC *slowly falls to his knees)*
Now, beg me to spare your life the way my son begged you to spare his.

BIG MAC
He didn't beg me to spare his —

AL
I said beg!

BIG MAC
He didn't beg me to spare his life.

AL

I said beg, goddamnit!
(Beating him with the gun butt)
Beg! Beg! Beg! Beg! Beg! Beg!... Beg!

(BIG MAC *is hunched over on the
floor, covering his head.)*

AL

I told you to beg! When I say beg, you don't ask questions,
you don't answer me back, boy, you beg! Hear me?
(Beat)
Do you hear me?

BIG MAC

Yes.

AL

What?

BIG MAC

Yes.

AL
(Hitting him again)
What?!

BIG MAC

Yes, sir!

(AL *finally returns to the chair.*
BIG MAC *is still hunched over.)*

AL

See what you made me do? Hurt my trigger finger. That's
how accidents happen.
(Kissing his sore finger)
Next time I tell you to do something, you do it.

> (BIG MAC *finally uncovers his face. He wipes his tear-filled eyes.*)

AL

I bet your daddy whips your ass all the time, don't he?
> *(Pantomiming dramatically)*

"Whap! Whap! Whap! Whap!" 'Cause you are one stupid little bastard.

BIG MAC

Stop calling me that.

AL

Make me.

BIG MAC

You think you all that 'cause you got a gun? Wait. Just wait 'til my popz comes home. He's gonna put a cap in your ass.

AL

Really?

BIG MAC

Hell, yeah!

AL

Know what I think? I think he's gonna thank me for doing what he's probably wanted to do to you for a <u>long</u> time.

> (BIG MAC *makes a mad rush for AL, who deftly dodges him and throws him to the ground.*)

AL

That was dumb.
> *(Looking down on him with a smile)*

Damn boy, ain't'chu good at anything besides killing?
> *(Pointing the gun at him)*

Get your ass back on the sofa.

(BIG MAC *slowly picks himself up and starts for the sofa.*)

AL

That's why I'm'a shoot your monkey-ass.

(AL *sits in the chair and carefully puts the gun on the table.*)

AL

Think I'm hiding behind this gun, don't you? Well, I'm not a coward like you, and I'm gonna prove it.

(AL *crosses back to the chair, sits and carefully puts gun on the table.*)

AL

Go ahead. Make your move.

(BIG MAC *waits a beat, then starts for the gun. AL blocks his path and throws him back on the sofa.*)

AL

You had your chance.
(Beat)
You can't be no athlete.

BIG MAC

Dude, are you gonna shoot me or what?

AL

Eventually.

BIG MAC

You startin' to get on my nerves.

                              AL

Good. May you get high blood pressure, heart disease and
diarrhea.

                           BIG MAC

Will you <u>please</u> shoot me?

                              AL

I'll shoot you when I'm ready.

                           BIG MAC

You don't know when to chill, just like your son.

                              AL

Shut up! You didn't even know my son.

                           BIG MAC

All I wanted was his gold. He wouldn't give it up. When I
tried to snatch it off his neck, he elbowed me in the face.
Broke my nose. Instead of jetting out, what does he do? He
bum-rushes me.

                              AL

You shot him in cold blood and you know it!

                           BIG MAC

We wrestled on the ground. Then "Blam! Blam!" I stood up.
He didn't.

                              AL

You shot him!

                           BIG MAC

The gun went off!

                              AL

You killed him!!

BIG MAC

It was an accident!!

AL

If it was an accident you wouldn't've brought a gun, you would've used your hands like a real man. So don't try and weasel your way out of it now. You killed him. <u>You killed him</u>. Now, it's Judgment Day.

BIG MAC

I didn't wanna shoot him.

AL

But you did.

BIG MAC

If I didn't shoot him, he would've shot me.

AL

Then you should've let him shoot you.

BIG MAC

But —

AL

— you didn't. So now, I have to do it. I just wish Randall was here with me to share this Kodak moment.

BIG MAC

Killing me ain't gonna bring him back.

AL

Save that sermon for the congregation, Reverend. This ain't about bringing him back, it's about <u>payback</u>.

BIG MAC

Can I die now?

AL

In a minute.

BIG MAC

No, I wanna die now!

AL

You'll die when I say you can die. It's <u>my</u> finger on the trigger, not yours.
(Beat)
Trying to dictate. Boy, I'll pistol-whip your monkey-ass!

BIG MAC

Man, how come you so violent?

AL

How come you killed my son?
(No response)
I rest my case.
(Beat)
There's nothing wrong with violence as long as you're serving the public good. And right now, I feel I'm doing the public a great service.
(Beat)
A lot of black folks are scared of violence; think an eye for an eye is wrong; that violence begets violence. But sometimes violence begets <u>deterrence</u>, especially in the absence of justice. Violence is the American way.

BIG MAC

You sound like a cop.

AL

For all you know, I am. For all you know, I'm Darryl Gates in blackface. So you know I don't give a damn about your monkey-ass.

BIG MAC

I don't look like no monkey.

AL

You look like whatever I say you look like. If I say you look like a seal, you look like a goddamn seal.

BIG MAC

If I was your son I'd've run away a <u>long</u> time ago.

AL

If you were my son, I'd've shot ya coming out of the birth canal. Saved myself a doctor bill, saved my family a heartache, and saved the world one big headache.
        (Beat)
Let me ask you a question.

BIG MAC

You got the gun.

AL

See. That's why you can't be nice to baby felons.
        (Beating him with the gun butt)
Don't get smart with me, boy. Now, when I ask you a question, you answer me, goddamnit. Do you understand?

BIG MAC
(Covering his head)

Yes.

AL
(Still beating him)

What?

BIG MAC

<u>Yes</u>.

                              AL
<u>What</u>?!

                              BIG MAC
Yes, sir!

                              (AL *returns to his chair.* BIG
                              MAC *is fighting back his tears.)*

                              AL
That hurt me more than it hurt you, but you asked for it.
Talkin' shit. Made me mad. Now, I'm gonna try and ask my
question again. This time, I don't wanna hear no lip, understand me?

                              BIG MAC
                   (Beat)
Yes... sir.

                              AL
That's better.
                   (Beat)
Where'd you get that gun?

                              BIG MAC
Same place you got yours.

                              AL
I'm grown, I can buy one. You can't.

                              BIG MAC
So.

                              AL
So, where'd you get it? Who <u>gave</u> it to you?

BIG MAC

Why you wanna know? So you can break into they house?

(AL grabs him by the throat.)

AL

Keep getting smart with me, boy, I'll break your damn neck.

BIG MAC

It was for protection.

(AL finally releases him.)

AL

Protection? From what? Your homework? What? Was it chasing you home after school, trying to beat you up?

BIG MAC

Yo, everybody at school be packin'.

AL

The only thing you should be packin' is a lunch.

BIG MAC

Man, this ain't the '50s.

AL

I don't care if it's the Stone Age. A 15-year-old ain't got no business walking around strapped. If you were from the 'hood I could maybe see, but you're from the suburbs— the snobbiest black hills in town.

BIG MAC

Man, you outta touch. You don't understand.

AL

No, <u>you</u> don't understand.

BIG MAC

No, you don't understand!
(Beat)
It's rough in them streets. You either strap or get capped and
I ain't gettin' capped for nobody.

AL

So you cap somebody else's child.

BIG MAC

Man, I told you, it was an —

AL

And I told you, I don't wanna hear it!
(Mimicking him)
"It's rough in them streets." What does your bourgeois ass
know about the street? You were born with a silver spoon in
your mouth.

BIG MAC

No I wasn't.

AL

Your parents are professionals, right?

BIG MAC

My momz works at the hospital.

AL

She's a professional.

BIG MAC

It's a job, all right?

AL

Nursing is a profession, son. A career. It's not "just a job." A job is something you <u>have</u> to do. A career is something you <u>choose</u> to do. I'm sure she went to college.

BIG MAC

Yeah, so?

AL

So, you don't <u>have</u> to go to college to have a job. She made a <u>choice</u>. A conscious decision, whereas having you was probably an accident. You know, it just happened.

BIG MAC

Man, why you sweatin' me?

AL
(Mimicking him)
"Man, why you sweatin' me?"

BIG MAC

You be buggin'!

AL

That better mean I'm bad.

BIG MAC

You need help, man. A psychiatrist or something.

AL

I don't need no damn psychiatrist. Hell, I work for the post office. I know I'm crazy.
(Beat)
What does your father do again?

BIG MAC
(Beat)
He bowls.

                              AL
What?

                              BIG MAC
Bowls.

                              AL
<u>What</u>?

                              BIG MAC
                    (Read my lips)
<u>Bowls</u>.

                              AL
Cleans toilet bowls?

                              BIG MAC
He bowls, man!

                              AL
That's right, your father's a pro bowler... like the guys I see on
TV on the weekends.
                    (Beat)
Ain't that a bitch. I didn't even know they let brothers do that
kind of stuff... He is a brother, isn't he?

                              BIG MAC
No, he's green.

                              AL
Alright, McRib.

                              BIG MAC
Of course, he is.

AL

How come he wasn't at the trial? I never saw him one time during those two weeks. Just your mother.

BIG MAC

He... he was on the road.

AL

I guess.
(Beat)
So, when he's doing his thing... that means he's gotta wear... that means he's gotta wear those funny-looking shoes every day, huh?

BIG MAC

He has his own shoes.

AL

Good, 'cause them some ugly-ass shoes. Where's he at now, practicing?

BIG MAC

He's on his way back here right now. Yeah. To take me to see my probation officer. Yeah.

AL

No, he's not. He's on tour. Playing in the Albuquerque Open, right?

(BIG MAC *looks at him, surprised.)*

BIG MAC

How did you...?

AL

A good killer does his homework.

(AL *stares at him, shaking his head, as he takes a swig.*)

BIG MAC

What?

AL

Nothing. I'm impressed.
(Taking another swig)
Not by you. By your parents. I wonder where they went wrong? Maybe it was a bad chromosome. A defective gene or something.

BIG MAC

Man, ain't nothin' wrong with me.

AL

You think. Let me ask you a question, since I've "got the gun": you think your parents are proud of you? I know they're not but just play along with me. Think they're proud of you?

BIG MAC
(Beat)
I don't know.

AL

Come on now, you know.

BIG MAC
(Beat)
Yeah, I guess.

AL

And then you woke up.

BIG MAC

Hey, you asked me a question, okay?

AL

Don't start, Filet o' Fish.

> (AL *puts the liquor bottle on the table.*)

BIG MAC

My name is Big Mac.

AL

What?

BIG MAC

I said, my name is Big Mac. Not Quarter Pounder, not Small Fry, not Happy Meal, not McRib, not Filet O' Fish, not mon-key-ass. Big Mac.

AL

Son, no parents in their right minds would name their child after a hamburger, I don't care how good it is.
> *(Beat)*
If you want me to call you by your name, I'll call you by your name — your <u>real</u> name.

BIG MAC

> *(Beat)*

Shawn.

AL

Shawn? That's a girls' name.

BIG MAC

It's a boys' name too.

AL

It's effeminate.

BIG MAC

It's my name!

AL

Then why don't you use it?!
(Beat)
Look, there's nothing wrong with your name; I'm just glad it ain't mine.

BIG MAC

Man, leave me alone.
(Beat)
Yo, can I get a swig?

AL

<u>May</u> I have a swig?

BIG MAC

<u>May</u> I have a swig?

AL

Please?

BIG MAC

Man, I ain't begging you.

(AL *savors the brim of the bottle.*)

AL

Boy, this is some good shit.

(AL *is about to take another swig.*)

BIG MAC

(Beat)
May I have a swig... please?

AL

No. I don't wanna contribute to the delinquency of a minor, even though you're already delinquent.

(Taking the last swig)

So, you think your parents are proud of you?

(No response, in his face)

You're a murderer. A cold-blooded, teenage killer. You ain't finished high school and probably won't; you ain't got a job and couldn't even if you wanted to 'cause you're underage. All you care about is the here and now: dressing like a gangsta, hanging with your homies, and trying to knock up as many "bitches" as you can. That's it. Life's grand.

(Beat)

Well, let me tell you something Shawn — and I'm sure you've heard this before — there's no future in that shit. It can only take you two places — jail or the grave.

*(Downing th remaining liquor
in the bottle)*

Are your parents proud of you? No, they're not proud of you. They've lost you.

*(Using his handkerchief to wipe his
fingerprints off the furniture)*

As a parent, I know what it feels like to lose a child so I can sympathize with them. I lost my son, physically; they've lost you, spiritually.

*(Crossing to wipe his prints
off doorknob)*

Either way it goes, you're both dead. Only my son can never come back to me. You, on the other hand, still have a chance.

(Crossing to the sofa)

Unfortunately, I'm taking it away.

*(AL moves behind BIG MAC, exe-
cution style, putting the gun to his
temple.)*

                    BIG MAC

Look, I'm sorry for what happened to your son.

                    AL

Too late.

                    BIG MAC

I didn't mean to kill him.

                    AL

Too bad.

                    BIG MAC

I made a mistake.

                    AL

You <u>are</u> a mistake.

                    BIG MAC

Ever since it happened, I've been going to church twice a
week, trying to get saved.

                    AL
              (Unimpressed)
Hallelujah.

                    BIG MAC

Okay... Let me ask you a question? Are you a Christian?

                    AL

Not today.

                    BIG MAC

Okay, okay... Say you kill me.

                    AL

I'm trying to.

BIG MAC

One day, you're gonna die too. When your soul goes up and the Lord asks why you took my life, what'chu gon' tell Him?

AL

The devil made me do it.

BIG MAC
(Desperately)
Come on, man, don't do this!

AL

Why not? Give me <u>one</u> reason why I should let you live — <u>one</u>!

BIG MAC

Because I'm young?

(AL cocks the barrel.)

BIG MAC

All right! All right! Because I can change!

AL

You... can change?
(Off BIG MAC's nod)
You mean like Malcolm X? Or Don King? Or that actor...

BIG MAC

Charles Dutton?

AL

Yeah. I don't think so. For every one of those guys there's a million other guys out there who'll never be nothin' but thugs.
(Beat)

You think you're the exception? You're the rule. You're not gonna change. You're just scared. But that's okay. Everybody's scared of dying. Even Jesus cried on the cross.

> *(BIG MAC closes his eyes as* AL *prepares to squeeze the trigger.)*

> *(SFX: The sound of a car pulling into the driveway.)*

                    AL

Who's that?

                    BIG MAC

Must be my momz.

> *(AL crosses to the window adjacent the front door and peeks out.)*

                    AL

It's only two o'clock.
          (Checking his watch)
She's supposed to still be at work.

                    BIG MAC

On Wednesdays she gets off early so she can take me to Bible Study.

> *(AL glares at the picture of Jesus.)*

                    AL

Damn!
          (Beat)
So I guess this is what they call "divine intervention."

                    BIG MAC

Divine what — ?

                              AL
Look it up. It means God saved your ass — for now.

> *(AL crosses to the other side of the
> room and opens the side window.
> He starts back for* BIG MAC,
> *pointing the gun in his face.)*

                              AL
But I'll be back... in a year. And if you ain't acting on a sit-
com, promoting fights or selling bean pies on the corner I'm
gonna finish what <u>you</u> started. You understand me, Shawn?

                          BIG MAC
Yes, sir!

> *(AL puts the empty liquor bottle in
> his back pocket, hides the gun in
> the spine of his back, crosses to the
> open side window, climbs out and
> gives* BIG MAC *a final look.)*

                              AL
Happy anniversary, punk!

> *(AL exits. BIG MAC falls back on
> the sofa, relieved. He reflects for a
> moment, then falls to his knees on
> the floor, hands reverently clasped,
> tearfully staring at the black Jesus
> hanging over the sofa.)*

(Black out.)

                         THE END